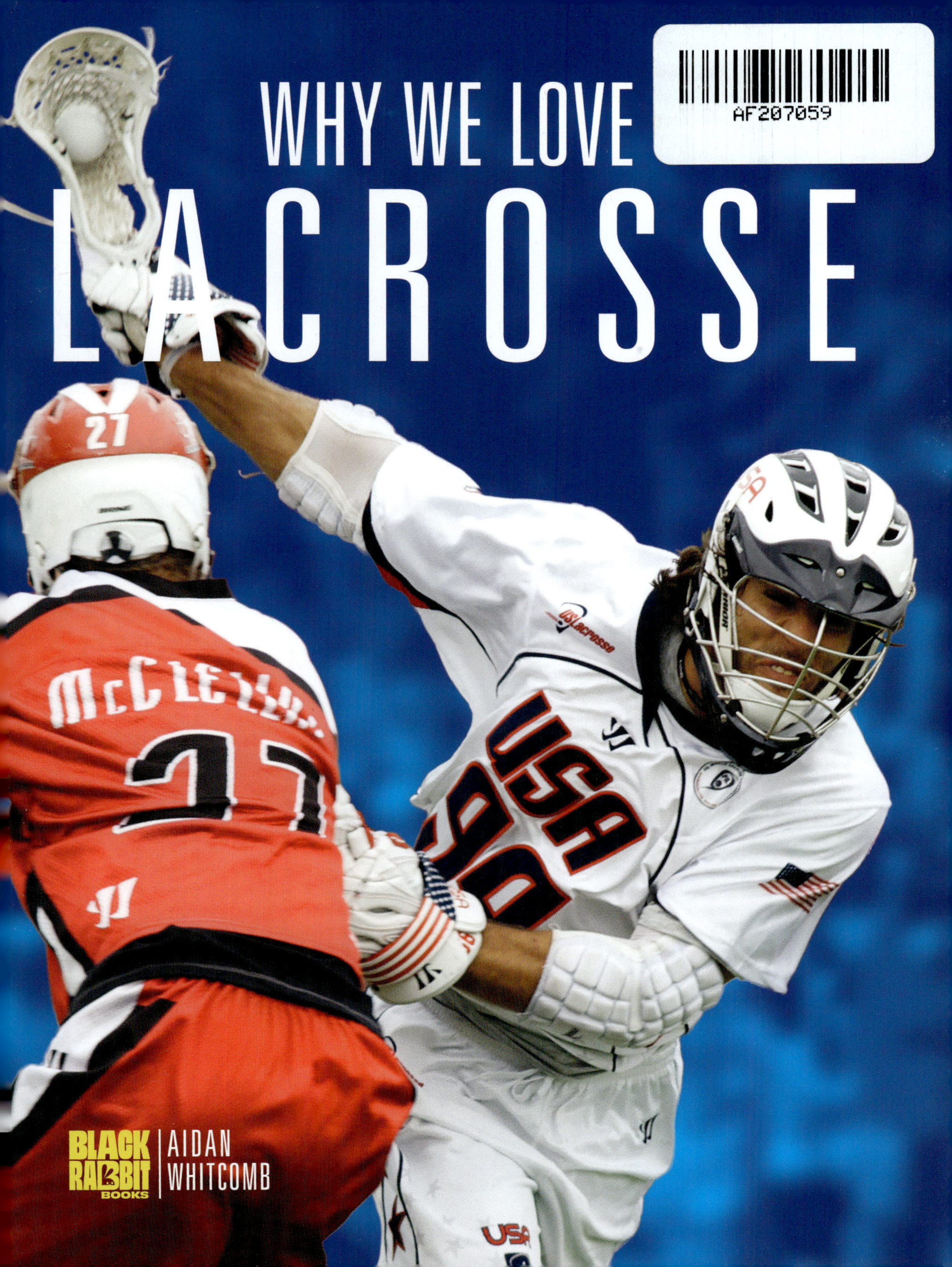

WHY WE LOVE
LACROSSE
AF207059
27
McCLELLAN
USA
BLACK RABBIT BOOKS | AIDAN WHITCOMB

TABLE OF CONTENTS

Ancient Origins

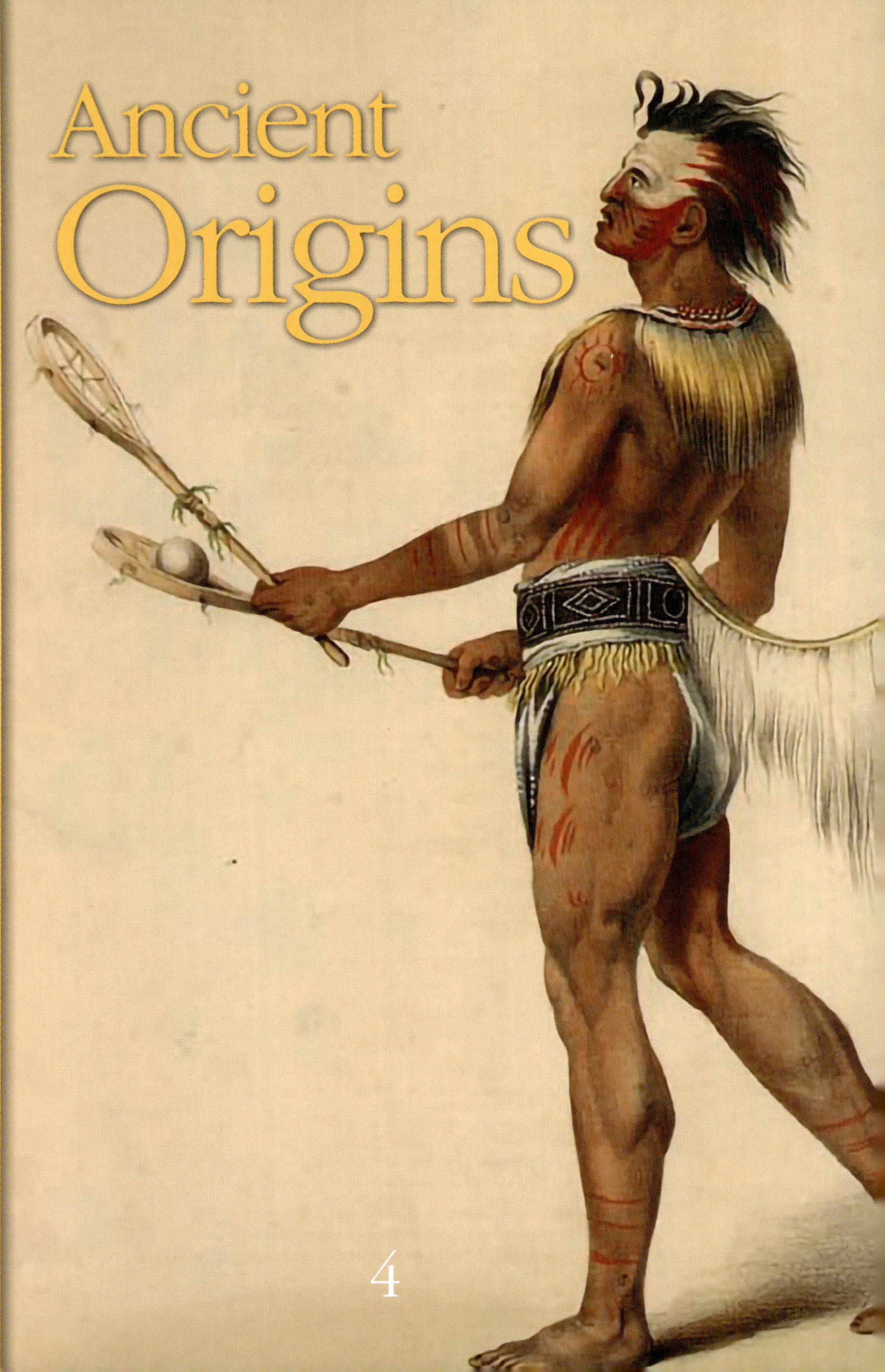

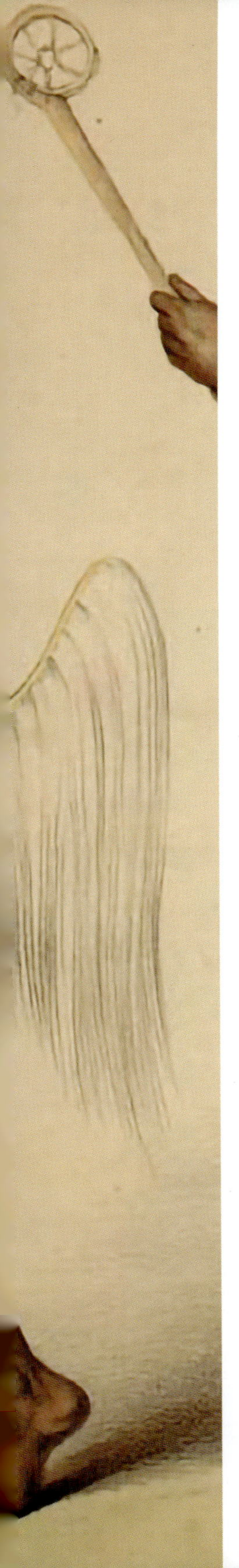

Lacrosse is an ancient game. It is the oldest sport in North America. American Indian communities created the game in the 1100s. Lacrosse is quite simple. Players use a stick to catch and pass a ball. They shoot at the goal. The game is very fast!

American Indians shared the sport with explorers. The sport began to grow. People in the United States and Canada loved the game. It became a popular high school and college sport. Today, it is played around the world.

Think About It

Research the history of lacrosse. How is the game played differently today?

Legends of Lacrosse

Paul Rabil

Lacrosse has many legends. Jim Brown is one of them.
He played for Syracuse University in the 1950s. Many
think he is lacrosse's GOAT. He was lightning quick
and extremely strong. He set many records.

Paul Rabil is another great player. He became
a professional in 2008.
He has the most
career pro points!

In the women's game, Charlotte North is
one of the best. She scored 358 goals in
college! Fans love to watch her play.

*Charlotte
North*

Did You Know?
Jim Brown also played in the NFL. He is in
the Hall of Fame for both lacrosse and football.

3

Sport of
Speed
9

Lacrosse is the fastest sport on two feet. Players sprint all around the field. They make quick passes. They avoid the defense. Fans love the speed of the game. The games are full of energy.

The goalie is an important position. They stop shots. Fans love it when a goalie makes a great save. Being a goalie is tough work. They must be quick. The goal is huge. And players shoot very hard. It can be scary in the net.

Think About It What skills does a great goalie need?

4

A Global
Game

Lacrosse has become a global game. In its early years, lacrosse spread to England and Australia. Now there are men's and women's leagues in multiple countries. The sport has gained many new athletes and fans.

The World Lacrosse Championship is a major tournament. Fans watch teams from around the world. Dozens of teams battle every four years. Smaller countries like Uganda and Jamaica can compete. It is an exciting event!

Did You Know?
The World Lacrosse Men's Championship is broadcast
in over 190 countries.

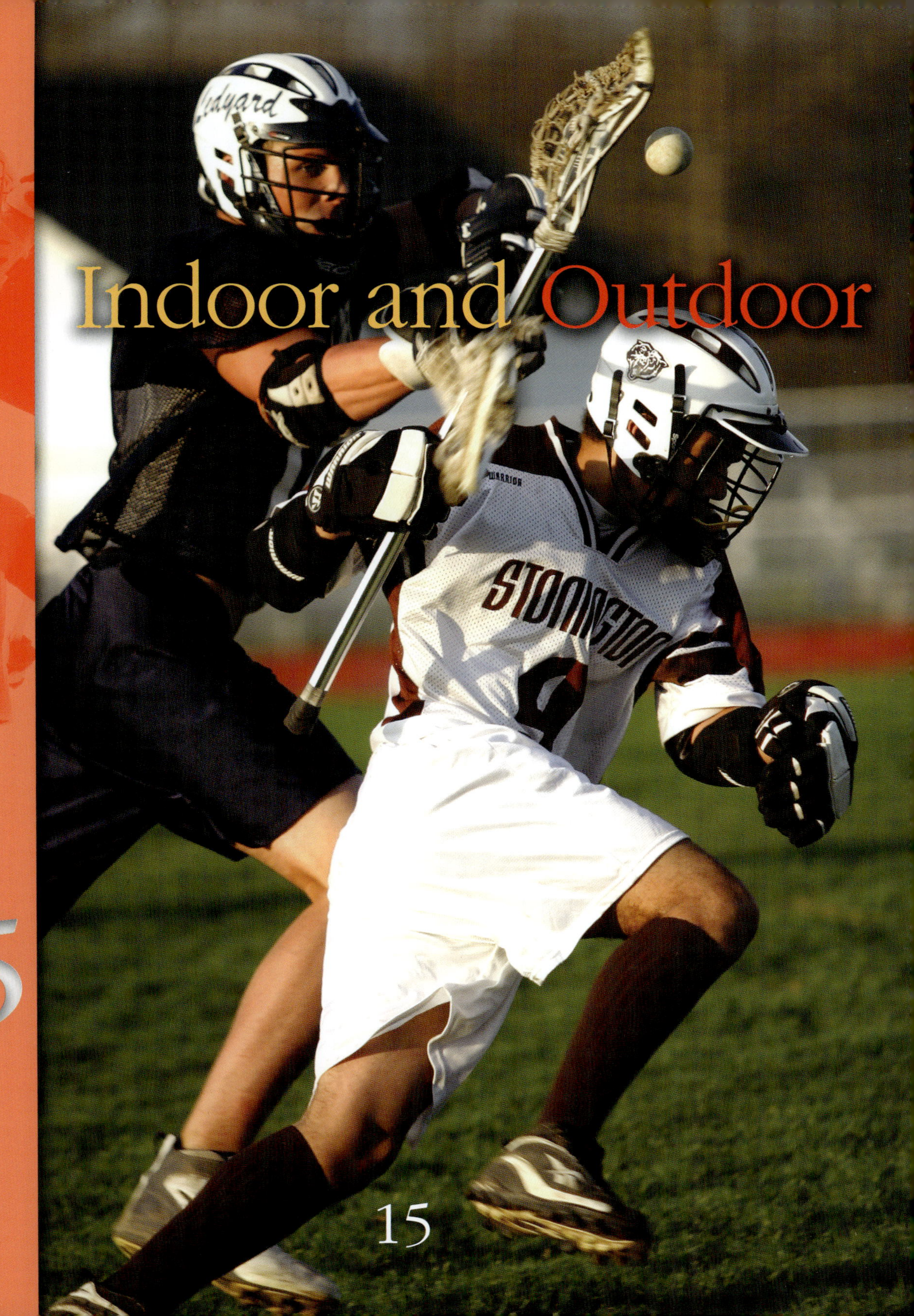

Indoor and Outdoor

5

Fans enjoy two main types of lacrosse. Field lacrosse is played outdoors. There is a lot of space to pass and run. Players shoot from all over the field. Fans enjoy the strategy of this game.

Box lacrosse is played indoors. The field is smaller. It is surrounded by boards. The game feels like hockey. Box lacrosse is more physical. It can be rough. Fans like to watch the strength of the players. Everyone enjoys the intensity.

PACIFIC
11
PACIFIC
5

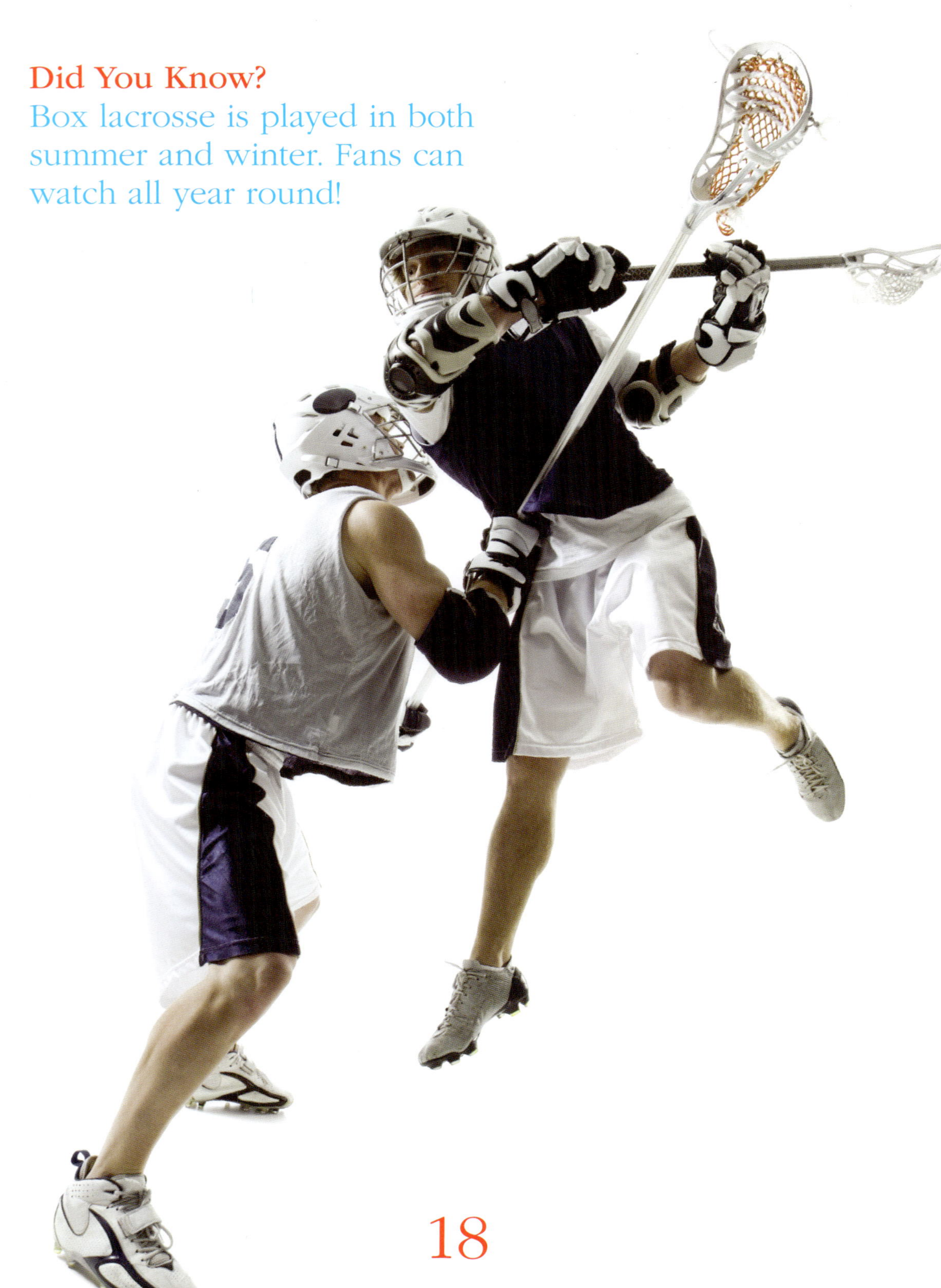

Did You Know?
Box lacrosse is played in both summer and winter. Fans can watch all year round!

Olympic Future

Lacrosse used to be in the Olympics. It was an event in 1904 and 1908. It was also a **demonstration sport** in 1928, 1932, and 1948. Then it went away for many years. It will be back at the Olympics in 2028. People around the world will watch the sport.

Olympians play a different version of the sport. It is called lacrosse sixes. It uses a smaller field. There are only six players per team. The United States and Canada are the two top countries. They have strong men's and women's teams.

Did You Know?
Canada won the Olympic gold medals
for lacrosse in 1904 and 1908.

FANTASTIC FACTS

Nick Diegel has the fastest shot at 127.4 miles (205 kilometers) per hour!

Lacrosse balls used to be made of wood or deerskin. Today they are made of rubber.

The US men's team has won 11 World Lacrosse Championships. The US women's team has won nine.

On average, players run about 3 to 5 miles (4.8–8 km) per game.

Lacrosse is a French word that means "the stick."

The Mohawk Lacrosse Club, started in 1868, is the oldest US team.

COOL COMPARISONS

Which colleges have the most championships?

(men's and women's combined, as of 2024)

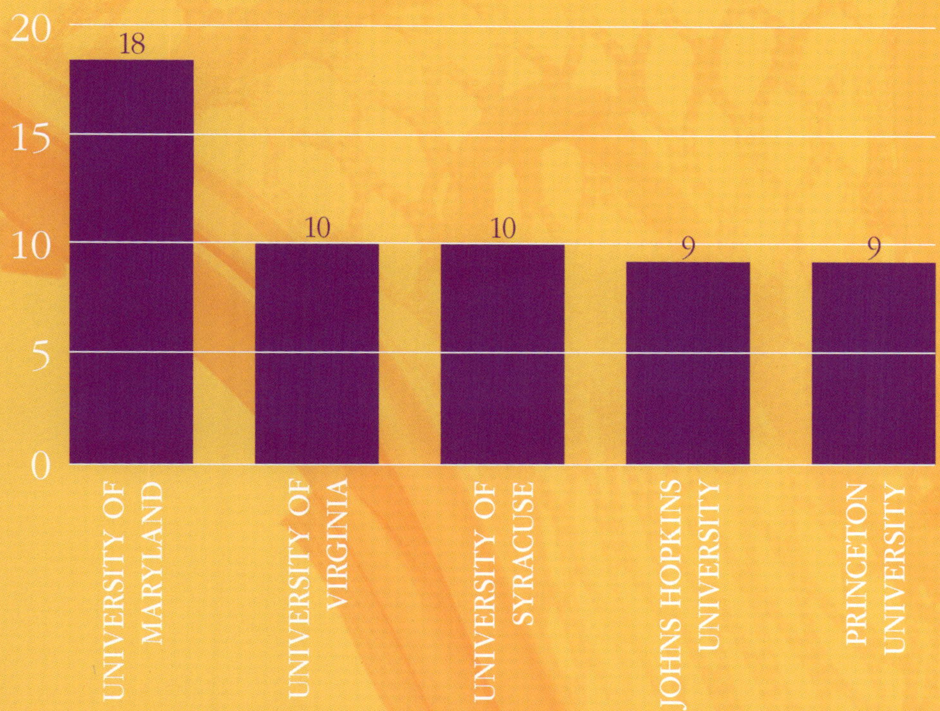

MORE TO EXPLORE
RESOURCES

Glossary

defense (DEE-fens) The players on a team who try to stop the other team from scoring.

demonstration sport (dem-uhn-STREY-shuhn SPAWRT) A sport that is played to create awareness, rather than to compete for medals.

draft (DRAFT) To pick a player for a professional team through a specialized system.

GOAT A person who is excellent or the best in their field; GOAT stands for "Greatest Of All Time."

league (LEEG) A group of sports teams that play against each other.

strategy (STRAH-tuh-jee) A careful plan or method.

tournament (TUR-nuh-muhnt) A series of matches between several teams, ending in one winner.

Read More

Berne, Emma Carlson. *Get Ready for a Lacrosse Game.* Minneapolis: Bearport Publishing Company, 2024.

Simons, Lisa M. Bolt. *Curious about Lacrosse.* Mankato, MN: Amicus, 2025.

Index

TOP RANK is published by Black Rabbit Books, P.O. Box 227, Mankato, MN, 56002. • COPYRIGHT © 2026 Black Rabbit Books. All rights reserved. No part of this book may be reproduced in any form without written permission from the publisher. • Top Rank is an imprint of Black Rabbit Books. • Designed by Danny Nanos • Photographs © Alamy Stock Photo/John Fryer, cover, 1; Dreamstime/Benjamin Haslam, 12–13, 23, James Boardman, 17; Freepik/alisaa, cover, 1; Getty Images/CDH_Design, 8–9, Erica Denhoff/Icon Sportswire, 7, M. Anthony Nesmith/Icon Sportswire, 6, 14, Paul Buckowski/Albany Times Union, 21; Rubberball/Erik Isakson, 2, 18, Xander Palaia, 11; Shutterstock/cobalt88, 14, JoeSAPhotos, 5, Larry St. Pierre, 14–15, Peyker, 10, Porstocker, 12, yojo626, 5; Wikimedia Commons/George Catlin, 4–5, Mack Male, 16, National Media Museum, 18–19, public domain, 20, 21 • Printed in India.

Library of Congress Cataloging-in-Publication Data: Names: Whitcomb, Aidan, author. | Title: Why we love lacrosse / by Aidan Whitcomb. | Description: Mankato, MN : Black Rabbit Books, [2026] | Series: Why we love sports | Includes bibliographical references and index. | Ages 8–11 | Grades 2–3 | Identifiers: LCCN 2024050026 | ISBN 9781644668061 (library binding) | ISBN 9781644668382 (paperback) | ISBN 9781644668702 (ebook) | Subjects: LCSH: Lacrosse—Juvenile literature. | College sports—Juvenile literature. | Classification: LCC GV989.14 .W52 2026 | DDC 796.36/2—dc23/eng/20241120 | LC record available at https://lccn.loc.gov/2024050026"